REPTILES ROCK!

INVESTIGATE!

I0798926

SNAPPING TURTLES EAT ANYTHING!

BY ELISE TOBLER

Enslow PUBLISHING

Please visit our website, www.enslow.com. For a free color catalog of all our high-quality books, call toll free 1-800-398-2504 or fax 1-877-980-4454.

Library of Congress Cataloging-in-Publication Data

Names: Tobler, Elise, 1970– author.
Title: Snapping turtles eat anything! / Elise Tobler.
Description: New York : Enslow Publishing, [2021] | Series: Reptiles rock! | Includes index.
Identifiers: LCCN 2019050664 | ISBN 9781978518346 (library binding) | ISBN 9781978518322 (paperback) | ISBN 9781978518339 (6 Pack) | ISBN 9781978518353 (ebook)
Subjects: LCSH: Snapping turtles—Juvenile literature.
Classification: LCC QL666.C539 T63 2021 | DDC 597.92/2—dc23
LC record available at https://lccn.loc.gov/2019050664

Published in 2021 by
Enslow Publishing
101 West 23rd Street, Suite #240
New York, NY 10011

Copyright © 2021 Enslow Publishing

Designer: Laura Bowen
Editor: Elise Tobler

Photo credits: Cover, p. 1 (snapping turtle) Yoaspermadi/Shutterstock.com; cover, pp. 1–32 (leaves border) Marina Solva/Shutterstock.com; p. 5 (photo) loki1982/iStock/Getty Images Plus/Getty Images; p. 5 (map) kateukraine/Shutterstock.com; p. 7 stockdevil/iStock/Getty Images Plus/Getty Images; p. 8 John Cancalosi/Oxford Scientific/Getty Images Plus/Getty Images; pp. 9, 25 Danita Delimont/Gallo Images/Getty Images Plus/Getty Images; p. 11 Rejean Bedard/iStock/Getty Images Plus/Getty Images; p. 12 sassy1902/iStock/Getty Images Plus/Getty Images; p. 13 arlutz73/iStock/Getty Images Plus/Getty Images; pp. 14, 15 Jupiterimages/Photos.com/Getty Images Plus/Getty Images; p. 17 Michael Duva/The Image Bank/Getty Images Plus/Getty Images; p. 19 martellostudio/iStock/Getty Images Plus/Getty Images; p. 20 Moondigger~commonswiki/Wikimedia Commons; p. 21 liveslow/iStock/Getty Images Plus/Getty Images; p. 23 File Upload Bot (Magnus Manske)/Wikimedia Commons; p. 26 Sista Vongjintanaruks/Shutterstock.com; p. 27 Yuriy Vahlenko/Shutterstock.com; p. 29 Daniel Parent/500Px Plus/Getty Images.

Portions of this work were originally authored by Kathleen Connors and published as *Snapping Turtles.* All new material this edition authored by Elise Tobler.

All rights reserved. No part of this book may be reproduced in any form without permission in writing from the publisher, except by a reviewer.

Printed in the United States of America

Some of the images in this book illustrate individuals who are models. The depictions do not imply actual situations or events.

CPSIA compliance information: Batch #BS20ENS: For further information contact Enslow Publishing, New York, New York, at 1-800-398-2504.

Find us on

CONTENTS

Words in the glossary appear in **bold** type the first time they are used in the text.

SNAPPERS

Snapping turtles look like animals that roamed while the dinosaurs were alive. Their squat bodies are covered with a hard shell. Alligator snapping turtles have spiked shells, while common snapping turtles have smooth shells. Both turtles have large heads with sharp beaks. That beak is made for biting, which is how snapping turtles got their name.

Snapping turtles live from the Rocky Mountains all the way to the East Coast of North America. They live in fresh water or brackish water, which is a mix of fresh and salt water. That usually means a river, pond, or lake.

GET THE FACTS!

There may be three different species, or kinds, of alligator snapping turtle. There's one species of common snapping turtle.

BIG BOYS AND GIRLS

Common snapping turtles can be as big as 19 inches (48 cm) long, and they can weigh up to 45 pounds (20 kg). Alligator snapping turtles can be up to 26 inches (66 cm) long and weigh up to 220 pounds (100 kg). In both kinds, males are larger than females.

A turtle's shell is called a carapace. The part of the shell that protects its belly is called the plastron. These shells protect the turtle's soft body. Snapping turtles have a smaller plastron than other turtles, so to keep safe, they snap their beaks at predators.

Snapping turtles have a hard shell, a spiky tail, and a beak for biting.

GET THE FACTS!

The spikes on an alligator snapping turtle's shell are called keels. The keels give the turtle extra protection from predators. No one wants to bite something so spiky! Turtle shells are hard and bony, like a suit of armor.

MUDDY WATERS

Snapping turtles really like muddy water. Mud helps them **camouflage** themselves from predators and while they hunt. They may hide in it with only their heads sticking out! Snapping turtles aren't ever found in very salty waters like oceans.

Snapping turtles don't like to leave the water, but they will to lay their eggs. They will also leave the water if they need to find a new place to live, sometimes traveling very long distances to do so.

This snapping turtle has come out of the water to lay in the sun.

GET THE FACTS!

Smaller turtles, like those you might keep as a pet, can pull their head and feet into their shell for protection. Snapping turtles are too big to do this.

COLD-BLOODED BEASTS

Snapping turtles, like most reptiles, are cold-blooded. This means that their bodies have no way of producing their own heat. They need an **external** source of heat. Snapping turtles will leave their watery homes to get warm on sun-warmed rocks or beaches. But what happens in winter?

In winter, snapping turtles will be very slow because there are fewer ways to stay warm. Snapping turtles do not **hibernate** in the winter. Snapping turtles can actually stay underwater all winter because they can breathe without using their lungs.

GET THE FACTS!

Snapping turtles don't just breathe through their lungs. Any kind of **muscle** that has a lot of blood vessels will do. In this way, turtles can breathe through their bottoms! This is helpful in winter.

LEAVE ME ALONE

Snapping turtles are solitary animals. This means they like to live alone. They are known for being **aggressive**. When they feel **threatened**, snapping turtles can also give off a bad smell. The snapping turtle is at the top of its food chain, meaning not many other animals try to eat it.

However, there are reports of river otters attacking snapping turtles. Coyotes, black bears, alligators, and even alligator snapping turtles may also prey on snapping turtles. The larger and older the turtle, the harder its shell is, so the better it is protected, or kept safe.

GET THE FACTS!

Snapping turtles have been taking over Japan, where they should not live at all. Snapping turtles are often brought in as pets for gardens and ponds, and then released when they become to hard to care for.

PREDATOR AND PREY

As a predator, snapping turtles will eat pretty much anything! They eat meat and plants, which means they are omnivores. They will eat other reptiles, birds, and small mammals. Snapping turtles will eat dead animals and even other turtles, which they do by biting their heads off.

Since snapping turtles live in rivers and ponds, you might imagine that they eat a lot of fish, and you would be right! Humans, also omnivores, will sometimes eat turtles. Humans have turned turtles into soup for hundreds of years.

This snapping turtle has caught a fish!

GET THE FACTS!

An omnivore will eat both meat and plants, while a herbivore eats only plants. Carnivores eat only meat.

GONE FISHING

Alligator snapping turtles have a very special tongue. The tongue has a small pink part that looks exactly like a worm. The snapping turtle will bury itself in mud and leave its tongue peeking out. When a fish comes to check it out, it gets eaten!

Alligator snapping turtles also have very strong **jaws**. You never want to be bitten by one because alligator snapping turtles can bite fingers right off.

GET THE FACTS!

The average life span of a snapping turtle in the wild is 30 years.

They can also chomp through broom handles and the shells of other reptiles, including other turtles.

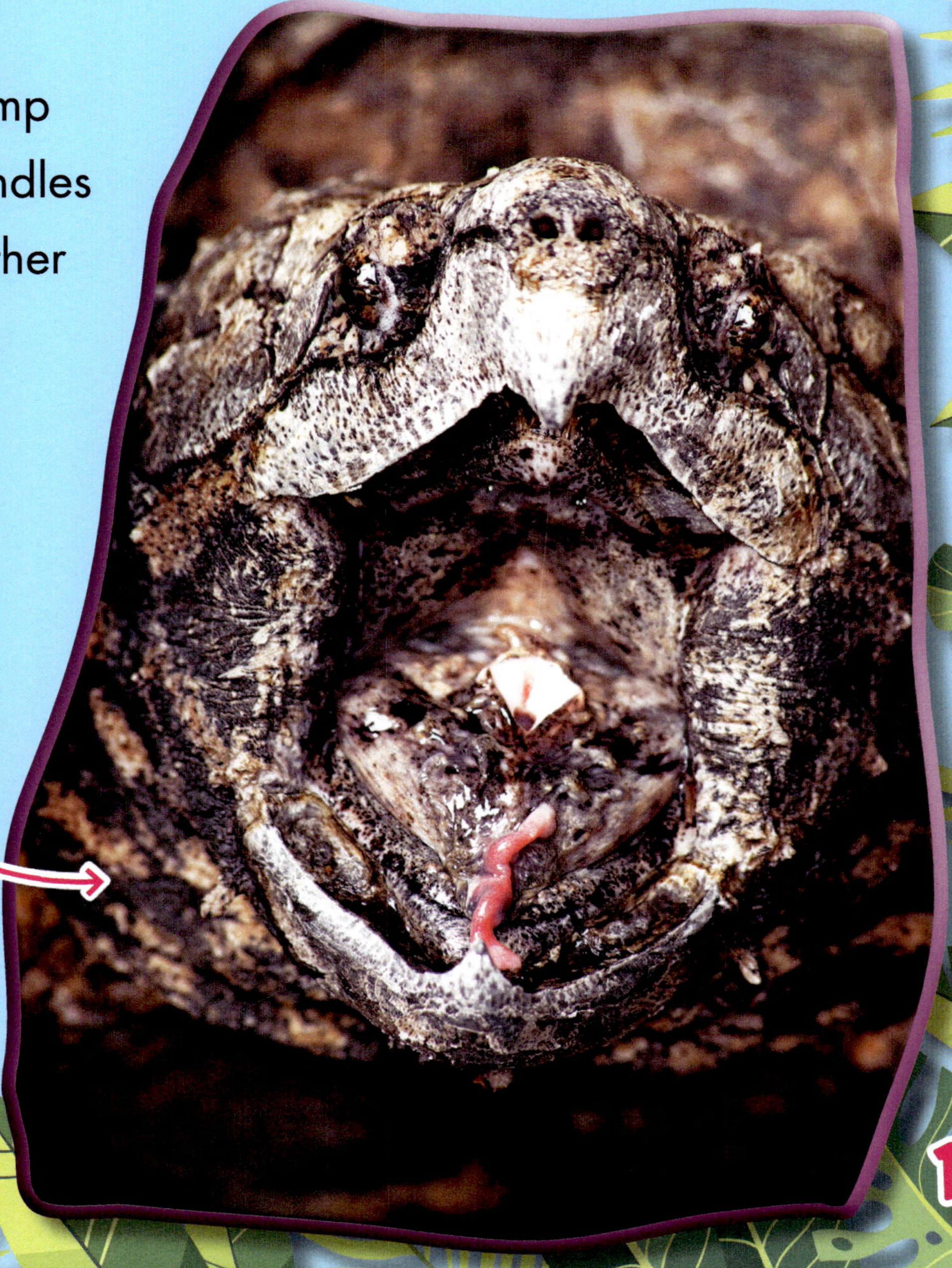

Here, you can see the pink part in the snapping turtle's mouth.

FAMILY MATTERS

Snapping turtles like to live alone, but when it's time to **mate**, they have to find other turtles. Snapping turtles usually mate between April and November, and they must come out of the water to do it. Female snapping turtles also make their nests on land.

Male snapping turtles will fight each other for the best females. The males will crash into each other like wrestlers, their battles lasting for up to an hour. They will bite and kick and scratch. They will stand up and roll each other around.

GET THE FACTS!

Female snapping turtles will build a nest to lay their eggs, but they won't be there when the baby turtles hatch. They cover up the eggs and go back to the water. Baby snapping turtles look for food and head for water when they're born.

BABY SNAPPERS

Female snapping turtles can lay up to 50 eggs each time. Eggs are often found and eaten by predators, so it's good there are so many. Female snapping turtles may return to the same place they built their last nest, walking up to 1 mile (1.6 km) to reach it.

Snapping turtle eggs are about the size of a golf ball. **Hatchlings** are born 80 to 90 days after the eggs are laid. They must break out of the shells and crawl up out of the nest. Baby snapping turtles are about 1 inch (2.5 cm) long at birth.

GET THE FACTS!

How hot or cold the eggs are will decide if the baby snapping turtle is a male or a female. Warmer eggs commonly become females. Colder eggs commonly become males.

This is a tiny baby snapping turtle!

DINOSAUR TURTLES

Turtles and snapping turtles have lived on our planet for 90 million years. Scientists have found **fossils** of snapping turtles that don't have the solid shells snapping turtles have today. But mostly, the turtles we know now are almost unchanged from those that roamed with the dinosaurs.

The American Museum of Natural History in New York has a fossil of the largest freshwater turtle to have ever lived. *Stupendemys* was probably 11 feet (3.3 m) long. It was probably so heavy it had trouble being a good swimmer, so it may have grazed on underwater plants.

This fossil of *Stupendemys* shows how large prehistoric turtles were.

GET THE FACTS!

It's almost impossible to know a snapping turtle's exact age, unless you saw it hatch, but you can make a guess by measuring its shell and counting the number of rings the shell has.

TURTLE RESCUE

Snapping turtles live in water more than out of it. However, there are times when you may see them walking from one pond or river to another one. You may see a turtle on the side of the road or in the road itself.

You should never pick up a snapping turtle. They may bite you, even if you pick them up by the sides of their shell. Sometimes, people have wrapped snapping turtles in blankets or tarps to safely move them. Shovels are also useful for scooping them up.

If you see a turtle in the road, take care with it.

GET THE FACTS!

Humans often try to capture snapping turtles. This is a bad idea. If you try to pick up a snapping turtle by its tail, you may badly injure it. It may also bite you!

NOT THE BEST PET

If you are thinking about keeping a snapping turtle as a pet, you might want to change your mind and consider a smaller turtle. Snapping turtles are so big that you would need to keep them in a child-sized swimming pool. You can't keep them inside.

GET THE FACTS!

Sometimes, a snapping turtle's shell will look extra green and fuzzy. Snapping turtles spend so much time underwater that plantlike living things called algae often grow on them!

Snapping turtles are usually nocturnal, meaning they are active at night. The best place to see a snapping turtle may be at your local zoo or aquarium. Zookeepers know how to keep snapping turtles safely, and zoos have enough room for them to move around.

This alligator snapping turtle is at home in an aquarium.

Not Yet Endangered

Like many animals in the wild, snapping turtles are losing their numbers because their **habitats** are in trouble. Pollution in rivers and ponds makes it hard for them to live. Many natural rivers and ponds have been drained to make way for farms too.

Snapping turtles aren't said to be endangered, or dying out, but many states have rules about the way people may deal with them. In the years to come, more rules may need to be made to keep them safe.

This snapping turtle is wearing a green coat of algae.

GET THE FACTS!

New York State made the common snapping turtle its official state reptile in 2006.

GLOSSARY

aggressive Showing a readiness to attack.

camouflage To blend in with one's surroundings.

external Coming from outside.

fossil The marks or remains of a plant or animal that formed over thousands or millions of years.

habitat The place where a plant or animal naturally or normally lives or grows.

hatchling An animal that has just hatched, or come out of an egg.

hibernate To be in a sleeplike state for an extended period of time, usually during winter.

jaws The bones of the face where teeth grow.

mate To come together to make babies.

muscle One of the parts of the body that allow movement.

threatened Something bad or harmful appears likely or possible.

FOR MORE INFORMATION

Books

Norsk, Caroline. *Snapping Turtles: Amazing Photos & Fun Facts Book About Snapping Turtles for Kids.* Scotts Valley, CA: CreateSpace Publishing, 2016.

Wilsdon, Christina. *Ultimate Reptileopedia: The Most Complete Reptile Reference Ever.* Washington, DC: National Geographic Children's Books, 2015.

Websites

BioKids Critter Catalog
www.biokids.umich.edu/critters/Chelydra_serpentina
Explore the world of the snapping turtle with the University of Michigan.

National Geographic
www.nationalgeographic.com/animals/reptiles/a/alligator-snapping-turtle
National Geographic takes you on a journey with snapping turtles.

The Smithsonian Zoo
nationalzoo.si.edu/animals/alligator-snapping-turtle
Our country's national zoo helps kids explore snapping turtles.

Publisher's note to educators and parents: Our editors have carefully reviewed these websites to ensure that they are suitable for students. Many websites change frequently, however, and we cannot guarantee that a site's future contents will continue to meet our high standards of quality and educational value. Be advised that students should be closely supervised whenever they access the internet.

INDEX